MAKING HOTROD RACERS FROM JUNK

MAKING HOTROD RACERS FROM JUNK

On your marks! With Tech-Nick and the rest of the team you will soon be up and running with five of your very own hotrod racers, ready to battle for pole position on the track.

Nick, RT-1, Databot and Nano will show you exactly how to turn recycled bits and pieces, from around the home, into some of the hottest vehicles in town.

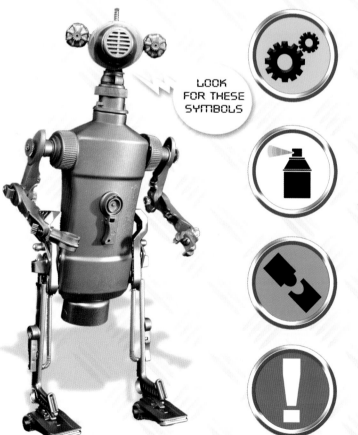

LOOK FOR THESE SYMBOLS

Parts Wherever you see this symbol you will find a box showing all the parts you'll need to collect, plus tips on finding alternatives to the ones shown.

Painting Learn from RT-1 about adding great paint effects and finishing touches. You will also see suggestions on where to apply the stickers found in the back of this book.

Assembly This section will show you how to construct each of the five featured hotrods using simple step by step instructions.

Red Alert Watch out for safety alerts, especially when using sharp tools.

Always ask an adult for help when advised to do so.

MAKING HOTROD RACERS FROM JUNK

CONTENTS

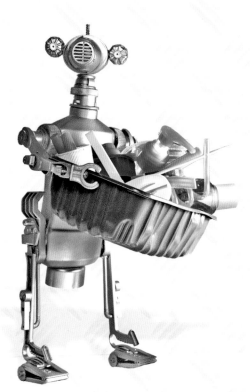

Start collecting junk today and it won't be long before you have enough parts to begin constructing cool cars and assembling awesome automobiles.

Ask others to help in your search for the right components. Friends and relatives may use different products around the home - see if they can help you find just what you're looking for.

Find a box to keep your recycled parts in and follow Nano's tips on page 5 for removing labels and cleaning them thoroughly.

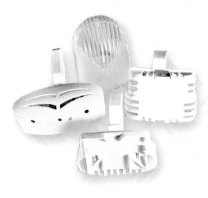

Jar lids and bottle tops make great wheels.

Toilet block holders can be used for front grills.

Use pen lids and wall plugs for exhaust pipes.

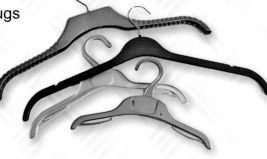

Coathangers are perfect for mudguards.

TE4M T4LK

Carefully peel off labels, starting in one corner and pulling evenly towards the other.

Use cream cleaner and scouring pads to remove stubborn labels or glue - then wash with clean water and leave containers and parts in a warm place to dry.

Cream Cleaner

Use strong adhesive to glue parts together. A glue gun is ideal, but ask an adult for help and wear protective gloves when using one. Hot glue only takes a few moments to cool and set.

Contact Glue Plastics

Contact adhesive bonds plastics well.
Glue both surfaces and leave to dry before pressing parts together. Use in a well ventilated room and get adult help.

SCORCH

First off the starting line is Scorch. Built from an antiperspirant roller, this hot vehicle will have every other contender sweating.

Track down the easy-to-find parts below and you'll be off to a flying start.

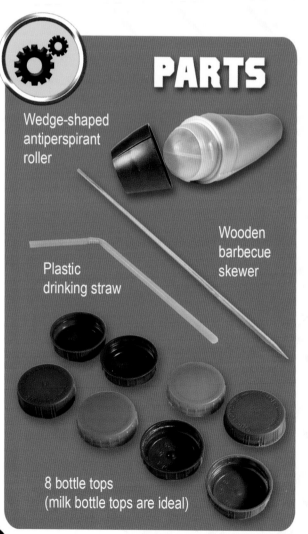

PARTS

Wedge-shaped antiperspirant roller

Plastic drinking straw

Wooden barbecue skewer

8 bottle tops (milk bottle tops are ideal)

TOOLS

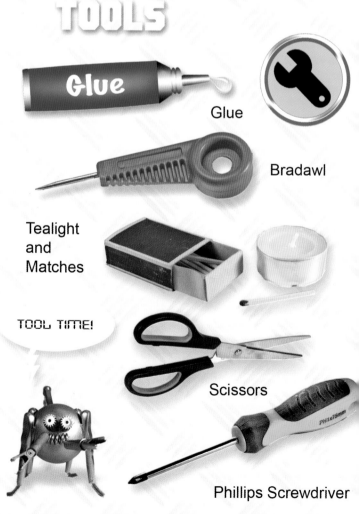

Glue

Bradawl

Tealight and Matches

TOOL TIME!

Scissors

Phillips Screwdriver

6

1

Heat a bradawl over a tealight flame for about 30 seconds.

Adult help recommended.

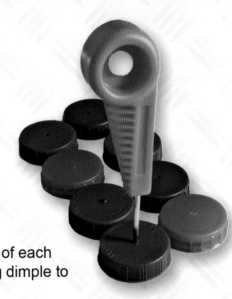

2 Pierce a hole with the heated bradawl in the centre of each plastic bottle top. There should be a small moulding dimple to show where this is.

Reheat the bradawl from time to time.

3

With a heated bradawl, pierce holes in both sides of the anti-perspirant roller along the seam lines as shown.

4 Push a Phillips screwdriver through the holes to widen them.

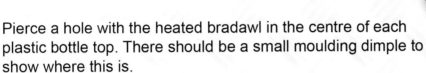

LINE UP THE
WHEELS CAREFULLY

5 Glue together the four sets of wheels and leave them to set.

5 Cut the barbecue skewer in half with scissors.

6 Cut four small pieces of drinking straw for wheel spacers - two about 1 cm long, and two about 1.5cm.

7 Slide skewers through the holes in the antiperspirant roller and fit the spacers with the longer pieces of straw on the front axle.

8 Slot all four wheels onto the axles and snip off the excess skewer.

Add a blob of glue to the end of each axle and allow to set.

Then paint the wheels and windscreen black and add stickers.

1

Here are some things you will need in order to set up your paintshop.
If the plastic containers you choose are already the right colour, there may
be no need to paint them. For a new overall colour use acrylic spray paints
and always follow the safety rules.

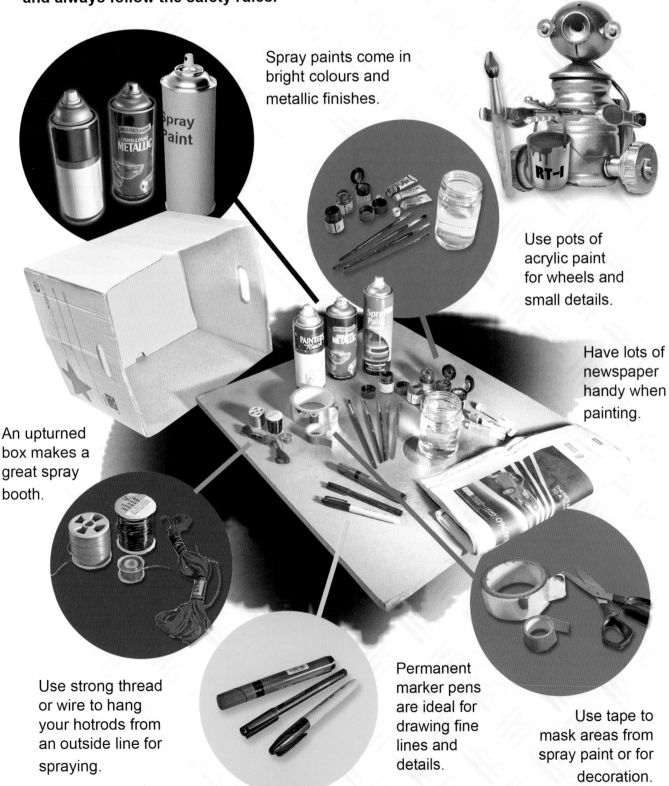

Spray paints come in bright colours and metallic finishes.

Use pots of acrylic paint for wheels and small details.

Have lots of newspaper handy when painting.

An upturned box makes a great spray booth.

Use strong thread or wire to hang your hotrods from an outside line for spraying.

Permanent marker pens are ideal for drawing fine lines and details.

Use tape to mask areas from spray paint or for decoration.

2 FAST TRAK

Fast, formidable and furious, that's Fast Trak.

Check out those mean exhaust pipes and awesome flames.

From zero to sixty in five seconds, this supercharged racing machine is a fireball.

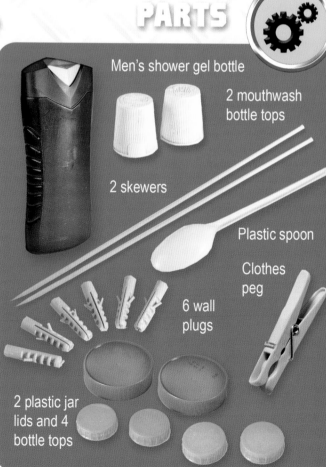

TOOLS

Glue

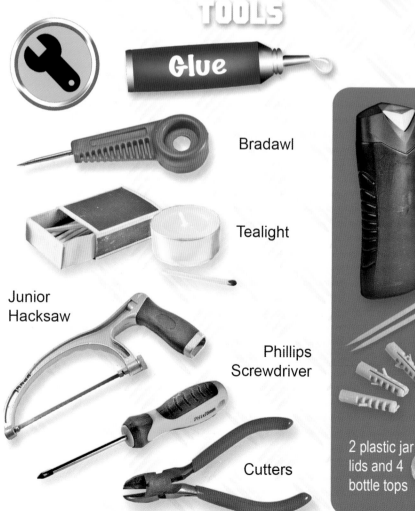

Bradawl

Tealight

Junior Hacksaw

Phillips Screwdriver

Cutters

PARTS

Men's shower gel bottle

2 mouthwash bottle tops

2 skewers

Plastic spoon

Clothes peg

6 wall plugs

2 plastic jar lids and 4 bottle tops

1

Use a heated bradawl to pierce holes in the centre of each jar and bottle lid.

Look for the centre dimple on the inside or outside of the lid.

Hold the point of the bradawl just above the flame to keep it from turning black.

Ask for help from an adult when heating tools.

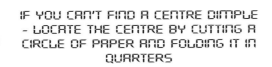

IF YOU CAN'T FIND A CENTRE DIMPLE - LOCATE THE CENTRE BY CUTTING A CIRCLE OF PAPER AND FOLDING IT IN QUARTERS

2

Use a heated bradawl to pierce holes in both sides of the shower gel bottle for the axles to fit through.

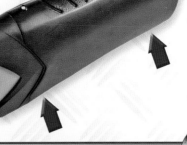

3 Use a Phillips screwdriver to widen each hole in the gel bottle so that the axles run smoothly.

4 Slide barbecue skewers through each axle hole and fit wheels to each side as shown.

5 Slide the wheels together and glue along the rims of the bottle tops.

Cut off the excess skewer with clippers before adding a blob of glue to the end of each axle.

6 Glue a plastic spoon to the top of the gel bottle as a canopy then snip off the excess handle with scissors once the glue has set.

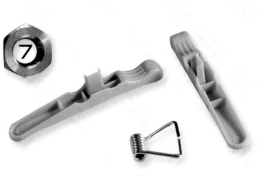

Pull apart the plastic clothes peg.

Glue a wall plug to the peg on an angle as shown.

⑨

Glue two more wall plugs to the peg and to each other as exhaust pipes.

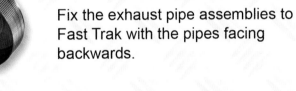

Prepare a second exhaust pipe assembly in exactly the same way.

⑩

Fix the exhaust pipe assemblies to Fast Trak with the pipes facing backwards.

Hang Fast Trak from a line for spraying, then paint the wheels, exhaust pipes and canopy with acrylic paints before adding stickers.

2

3 Nitromatic

With a long wheel base and low profile, Nitromatic scorches ahead powered by an awesome nitrous oxide engine.

HYDROMATIC
SYSTEMATIC
NITROMATIC!

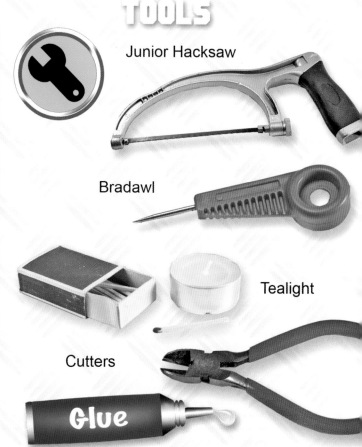

 **PARTS**

Collect all the parts and tools shown on this page, then check out the workshop pages to see how it's built.

TOOLS

Coathanger

Spray bottle top

Barbecue skewers

Shampoo bottle lid

Soap bottle

2 jar lids, 4 bottle tops and 2 pop-up tops

Two pen tops

Junior Hacksaw

Bradawl

Tealight

Cutters

Glue

1

Saw the arms from the plastic coathanger with a junior hacksaw.

Ask for adult help when using a hacksaw.

2

Unscrew the soap bottle top and pull out the short plastic tube.

Keep the tube in a safe place for later.

3

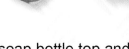

Glue

GLUE THE ENDS
AND SIDES WELL

5

Replace the soap bottle lid and glue a coathanger arm to each side of it.

Remove the tube from a spray bottle top and pierce holes through both sides of the rotating collar.

A skewer should be able to slide through easily.

4

Heat a bradawl over a tealight flame for about 30 seconds.

Adult help recommended.

⑥

Glue the spray bottle top to the other end of the coathanger arms.

Take care at this stage to keep both hanger arms straight and level.

If one side of Nitromatic is higher than the other, the wheels will not sit on the ground evenly.

⑦

Using a heated bradawl, pierce holes though the centre of each jar lid and bottle top. Holes should be just large enough for a skewer to fit through tightly.

Most tops will have a small moulding dimple to indicate the exact centre. Reheat the bradawl from time to time.

⑧

Slide bottle tops along the barbecue skewers.

Glue around the rim of the smaller tops and push the wheels together as shown below.

⑨

Pierce a hole in each side of the soap bottle with a heated bradawl.

Make the holes large enough for the skewers to fit through easily.

!

Always ask for adult help when heating tools.

10 Push the rear wheel assembly through the holes in the soap bottle and thread a bottle top and jar lid onto the opposite side.

Glue

11

Glue the rim of the bottle top to the jar lid and snip off the excess skewer. Leave a gap between the wheels and the soap bottle so that they can spin freely.

MAKE THE
SPACERS ABOUT
ONE CENTIMETRE

12 Snip two small pieces from the soap bottle tube that was removed at Stage 2.

These will be used as spacers to help the front wheels spin easily.

13

Push the front wheel assembly through a spacer and the holes in the spray bottle - then thread a spacer and bottle tops onto the other side.

DON'T GLUE THE
SPACERS!

14

Glue

Glue the smaller cap inside the larger bottle top and snip off the excess skewer.

Make sure that the wheels spin freely.

15 Glue on the shampoo bottle top for a canopy.

16

Glue pen tops to the back of Nitromatic for exhaust pipes.

PAINTSHOP TIPS

1 Stick tape over the windscreen canopy before spraying.

2 Hang Nitromatic on an outside line using strong thread or fishing line.

SHAKE THE PAINT CAN WELL

Short spray bursts will avoid paint runs.

Let the paint dry for a few moments before addin *more layers.*

3 When dry, paint the wheels with black acrylic paints.

3

4 Remove the tape fr the windscreen and add Nitro's stickers

4 TURBOTRON

Turbo-charged and tuned for top performance, this hotrod is a scorcher.

Extra wide wheels ensure maximum traction and a super streamlined body cuts down on wind drag.

TOTALLY TURBOTASTIC!

TOOLS

Junior Hacksaw

Bradawl

Glue

Cutters

Tealight and Matches

PARTS

A small skirt hanger

2 large jar lids

6 wall plugs

2 barbecue skewers

2 fresh juice bottle tops

Spray bottle

Highlighter pen top

4 juice bottle tops

ASK AN ADULT
FOR HELP
WHEN USING
SHARP TOOLS

1 Remove the plastic tube from the spray bottle top and pull out the inside collar with pincers.

2 Glue the nozzle of the spray bottle top into the neck of the spray bottle, keeping it perfectly straight.

Glue

3 Heat the tip of a bradawl over a tealight for about 30 seconds.

4 Pierce holes in both sides of the spray top collar for the wheel axle to fit through.

5 Use a Phillips screwdriver to widen the hol

20

⑥ Pierce holes in both sides of the spray bottle for the rear wheel axle to fit through.

WIGGLE THE SCREWDRIVER ABOUT TO DO THIS

⑦ Widen the holes with a Phillips screwdriver.

Use a heated bradawl to pierce holes in the centre of each jar lid and fresh juice bottle top.

⑧

⑨

Make holes in each of the four pop up juice bottle tops.

⑩

Reheat the bradawl several times when making holes. Dip the point in cold water to make it safe afterwards.

IF THE TOPS YOU ARE USING ALREADY HAVE TWO HOLES, CAREFULLY PIERCE A HOLE IN BETWEEN

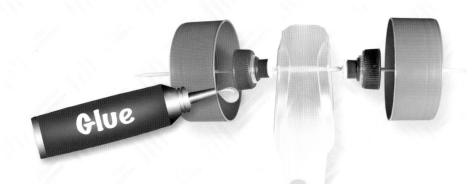

11 Slide a barbecue skewer through the rear axle holes, then fit the bottle tops and jar lids as shown.

Glue the rims of the juice bottle tops to the jar lids, making sure that the wheels are not too tight against the sides of the spray bottle.

12 Once the glue has dried, cut off the excess skewer.

IF THE WHEELS ARE TIGHT AGAINST THE BOTTLE THEY WON'T SPIN

13 Slide a skewer through the front axle holes and glue the wheels together as shown.

14 Snip off the excess skewer with scissors or cutters.

15 Saw the hook from the plastic skirt hanger.

! *Always rest on a firm worksurface when cutting.*

TRY TAPING PARTS IN PLACE WHILE THE GLUE SETS

16 Glue the hanger to the top of the spray bottle with its clips facing backwards.

Glue

17 Glue the highlighter pen top to the front of Turbotron with the open end facing forwards as an air intake.

Glue

18 Glue six wall plugs to the sides of the air intake with the open ends angled upwards for exhaust pipes.

Glue

Glue

19 Fix juice bottle top caps to the sides of Turbotron for headlamps.

PAINTSHOP

Find a suitable place outdoors to spray paint. Wait until the paint is completely dry before adding stickers, or they may peel the paint off.

1 Cover Turbotron's headlamps with small pieces of kitchen cling film or foil to protect them from paint during spraying.

Adult help recommended

2 Spray several thin coats of paint to avoid runs.

3 Paint the wheels black and engine silver with acrylic paints.

4 Carefully remove the cling film from the headlamps and add stickers.

Spray Paint

4

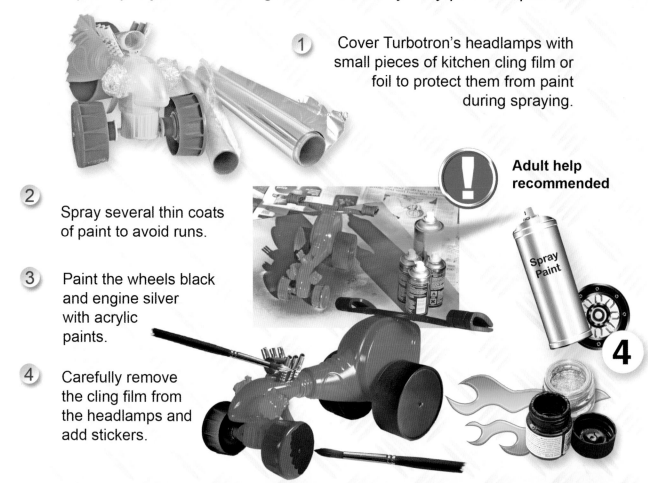

DATA's FACTSTOP

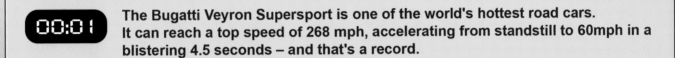

00:01 The Bugatti Veyron Supersport is one of the world's hottest road cars. It can reach a top speed of 268 mph, accelerating from standstill to 60mph in a blistering 4.5 seconds – and that's a record.

00:02 RAF fighter pilot, Andy Green, broke the world land speed record on October 15th 1997. Driving in his Thrust SSC (Supersonic Car) he reached a top speed of 763 mph in the Black Rock Desert, Nevada USA. It was also the first time that anyone had broken the sound barrier in a car.

00:03 Hotrod cars, short for Hot Roadsters, became very popular in the 1930s and 1940s. Built from junkyard parts, they were used for racing across the sandy Californian deserts and dry salt flats.

00:04 The first ever automobile race was back in 1894. Twenty five cars set off from Paris and chugged to the finish line in Rouen, 79 miles away, travelling at an average speed of just 12 mph. The winning car was a Peugeot, driven by Georges Lemaître.

00:05 Dragsters run on Top Fuel – a mixture of nitric acid and propane. With engines that can generate 7,000 horse power, they accelerate to 100 mph in less than 0.7 seconds and can reach speeds of over 300 mph.

00:06 The World's longest race track is 17 miles from start to finish. Built on the island of Gotland in Sweden, it is longer than the Nürburgring 'Green Hell' Grand Prix track in Germany by a mile.

00:07 George Schuster was the winner of the longest car race in history. After 169 days and 22,000 miles, he drove in to Paris in his Thomas Flyer automobile back in 1908, after crossing the USA's open prairies, endless miles of frozen Siberian mud and bumpy roads of Europe. He beat the next fastest car by 26 days.

00:08 Pit stop crews of up to 19 mechanics can swap tyres, replace parts, remove debris and refuel a racing car in around 7 seconds. Fuel is pumped into the tank at a rate of 12 litres per second.

00:09 Danica Patrick became famous on April 20th 2008 as the first woman driver to win an IndyCar race at the Twin Ring Motegi track in Japan – beating Brazilian driver, Helio Castroneves, who ran out of fuel on the last lap.

00:10 Brooklands in Surrey, England, was the first ever purpose-built motor racing track. The 3 mile course opened in June 1907 and was made of concrete.

Topped up with gallons of grunt, this hotrod is a raging bull of a racing car.

Built from an old oil container, it has a cool front air grill and rear fins.

Collect the parts and tools shown below and start crafting.

SNARLTASTIC

PARTS

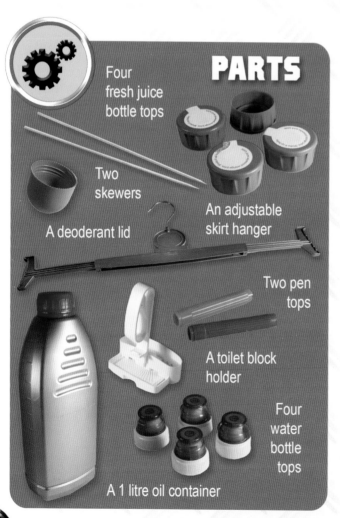

Four fresh juice bottle tops

Two skewers

A deoderant lid

An adjustable skirt hanger

Two pen tops

A toilet block holder

Four water bottle tops

A 1 litre oil container

TOOLS

Tealight and matches

Scissors

Bradawl

Phillips Screwdriver

Junior Hacksaw

Cutters

! *Adult help recommended*

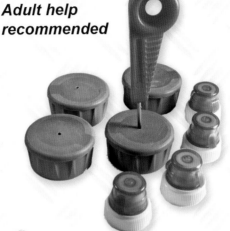

(1)

Heat the tip of a bradawl over a tealight for about 30 seconds.

(2)

Pierce holes in the centre of each bottle top with a heated bradawl.

Leave the caps on the water bottles when doing this.

(3)

Glue the four water bottle tops inside the juice bottle tops to make the wheels.

 Glue

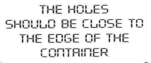

(4)

Pierce holes in the oil container with a heated bradawl for the axles to fit through.

THE HOLES SHOULD BE CLOSE TO THE EDGE OF THE CONTAINER

(5) Use a Phillips screwdriver to widen the axle holes.

(6)

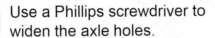

Pass the barbecue skewers through the oil container and fit the wheels.

Leave a small gap to allow the wheels to spin freely.

7 Snip off the skewer ends with cutters and add a blob of glue to the end of each axle.

8 Glue pen tops to the back of Road Rage as exhaust pipes.

9 Cut the hook from the toilet block holder with scissors.

10 Glue the toilet block holder to the front of Road Rage as an air grill.

WASH THE TOILET BLOCK HOLDER WELL FIRST

11 Saw the ends from an adjustable skirt hanger.

12 Glue the sawn-off hanger ends to the back as stabiliser fins.

13 Draw a line with a marker pen dividing a deoderant lid exactly in half.

KEEP A
STEADY HAND

14 Saw the deoderant lid in half, carefully following the line you have drawn.

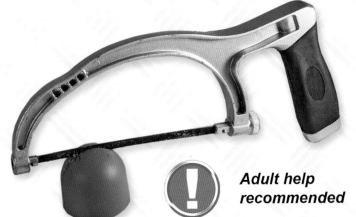

 Adult help recommended

15 Glue one half of the deoderant lid to the top of Road Rage as a canopy for the driver.

Give Road Rage a coat of paint, paint the wheels black and add stickers.

CHAMPION'S CUP

Make a winner's trophy and award it to the fastest car in your team.

All you need are two yoghurt pots, two plastic coathangers and a cork. Then spray with paints and let the race commence.

A Cork

Two Yoghurt Pots

Two Plastic Hangers

2 Saw the hooks from the two plastic hangers.

1 Glue the cork to the yoghurt pot bases.

Glue

3 Glue a hook to each side of the cup.

Glue

Spray Paint

Black
ACRYLIC PAINT

4 Spray your trophy with metallic paint, then paint a black band around the base.

 # GLOSSARY

Accelerate
To increase in speed - to go faster.

Acrylic paint
Fast drying paint that can be diluted in water, but is waterproof when dry.

Antiperspirant
A chemical that you put on the skin to reduce sweating.

Axle
The shaft on which a set of wheels turns.

Barbecue skewers
Long thin sticks of wood used for holding pieces of meat together whilst cooking.

Bradawl
A pointed tool used for making screw holes.

Canopy
The glass window that covers the seat where a driver sits.

Customise
To alter or improve a vehicle by adding or taking away parts.

Dragster
A vehicle designed for drag racing in which two cars race in a straight line.

Horsepower
The measure of an engine's power. Also called Brake Horsepower.

Indycar
A type of single seat racing car named after the Indianapolis 500 race.

Nitrous Oxide
A gas used in dragster engines.

Pole Position
The lead position on the inside track.

Recycle
To reuse waste materials, or to alter them in some way for another purpose.

Supersonic
Faster than the speed of sound waves through air.

Tealight
A small candle in a metal holder.

Turbocharger
Part of an engine, driven by the exhaust, that makes it go faster.

Wheelbase
The distance between the axles.

First published in Great Britain in 2012 by Junkcraft Books. Email info@junkcraft.com
Text and Images © Junkcraft Books 2012. Stephen Munzer has asserted his rights under the Copyright, Designs and Patents Act, 1988, to be identified as the author of this work.

Designed and produced exclusively for Junkcraft Books.
Printed and Bound by Everbest Printing Co Ltd, China.

A CIP catalogue record for this book is available from the British Library.
ISBN 978-0-9571566-1-6

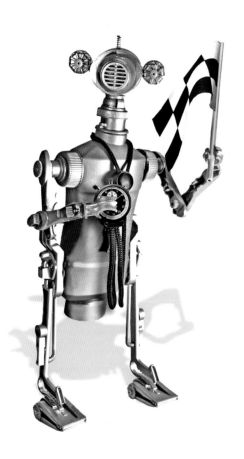

www.junkcraft.com

1 1

2

2

3 3 5 5

4

4

Nitromatic Nitromatic